THE MYSTIC ROSE

Alan Robinson

The Mystic Rose

ST PAULS

ST PAULS
Morpeth Terrace, London SW1P 1EP, United Kingdom
Maynooth, Co. Kildare, Ireland

© Alan Robinson, 1998

ISBN 085439 525 3

Cover illustration by Bill Armstrong

Produced in the EU
Printed by The Guernsey Press Co. Ltd, Guernsey, C.I.

ST PAULS is an activity of the priests and brothers of the Society of St Paul who proclaim the Gospel through the media of social communication

CONTENTS

Section One
FIRST APOCALYPSE   7
   Before the Beginning   9
   The Star Maker   15
   The Dream Maker   19
   Breasting the Sunlight   26

Section Two
THE FOUNTAIN OF LOVE   31
   Prologue   33
   The Petals of the Rose   36
   Straws Blowing in the Wind   40
   Scorching the Butterfly   44
   The Angel Stairs   48
   The Soul Healers   52
   Grace Upon Grace   56
   Centre of Flame   60
   The Cloud of Beauty   64
   A few worthwhile thoughts   68
   To Rent for Joy   72

Section Three
THE TAPESTRY   77
   At Ashness Bridge   79
   The Thames at Abingdom   80
   Stonehenge   81

Wordsworth and Coleridge in the Quantocks	82
The Quarry	83
Swallows Beside the Bridge	84
Kingfisher	85
St Richard's Bridge	86
Devil's Dyke	87
In the Bishop's Garden, Chichester	88
The Piper Tapestry, Chchester	89
At the Roman Palace, Fishbourne	90
Evening Over the Downs	91
Under the Bridges	92
Easter	93
Bread and Board	94
Section Four	
TWO TRILOGIES	95
Three Love Poems	97
I long to walk with you	99
Constant love	100
Love's old song	101
Three Autumn Poems	103
Love's season	105
Late afternoon in October	106
November 1st	107

Section One

FIRST APOCALYPSE

1
Before the Beginning

One still light, unchanging, ever burning,
never ending, never flickering:
there love lives its steady flame,
beyond the twilight worlds of time and space;
and in each universe of given breath,
Alpha and Omega turning
every dawn and every evening,
where Christlit resurrections snuff out death.

Node of thought, creating, ever changing,
tides of silver, ebbing, flowing, endlessly
upon the shores of galaxies;
the rainbow on the storm riding,
grasping the edge of what infinity reveals;
to new horizons arching,
as the twisting stars hurl across
those vast, eternal seas.

At the centre of all being, unbounded,
where whispered word with silence merges;
concealed behind bright walls of holiness,
where even hosts of seraphim are struck with awe;

there, power unfolding, all creation surges
out of the opening bud of ever love,
out of the mystic rose flowing,
teasing with heaven's fragrance
the bare room of here and now.

There is,
not an abstract beauty, but an outward blading,
from the thought and sense thrusting,
to hammered bronze and sonnet lines beating,
formed in the colour of each season's tree;
this is the man and woman kissing dusk to dawn,
and striding down the years uncounted
to the Eden gardens of the golden age,
renewed and Adam-naked, all time falling free.

Sinple truth unfurled, in many tongues
     outspoken,
all that is in word and being fashioned;
sword of sunshine, light in flesh enshrined,
all truth that fractures falsehood at the stem;
one silken cord of many strands, unbroken,
unfrayed by many time-spaced deeds in Godly
     mansions;
one truth to live by, heaven sending always
in the facets of a single, gleaming gem.

And in the glass of love, all good reflecting,
the soul from God is moulded in wet clay;

the goodness never falters,
but the flesh is weaker than the spirit given;
good intentions grasp the loving hand, but
    slipping,
slide to nothingness, to darkness falling;
yet in the palm of God nothing good is lost –
hell's paving is the lonely road to heaven.

Spirit, Father, Child in God, begetting
sons and daughters in the lovelit warmth of being;
the I am breaking into earthy song, longliving
and renewing in the dark womb's lullaby;
the One who is, who comes all coming,
goes all going – filters down the generations
to the dayspring doorway into life,
never one forgetting in the first searching cry.

Out of the One:
possibilities, sprung from the womb, sharing the
    glory,
million made and millions the more so;
onward, ongoing, outward giving,
all bountiful with many handedness;
universe on universe, chancing and changing,
peopled and more peopled, time and time again;
multicoloured on the rim, as newly as dawn
    comes,
always greater the store barns, never ever the less.

Atoms go whirling, thoughtless and empty,
shaping the stones, raising the cliffsides;
and out of the mind-lord the spirit breathes fire,
blows on dead clay and raises a child;
the thought forms go whirling into those atoms,
mind over matter churning out words,
in a flurry of brain fleeces breezing,
wind on the mountain, forest and field.

Out of the One:
images power all minds, make all dimensions,
each universe varied as skyscapes turning, star
     foraging,
down in the sunlit forest glades, touching
with whispering words the leaves on the bough;
measured apocalypse, roof tops all gleaming,
rain tumbled roses grown over with arches of
     song;
and far in the all making dream, the nerve centre
spreads to the edge of the where and the when and
     the how.

Before all beginning, after all ending,
the One is aware, all knowing, unbound in the
     boundless;
neither a now nor a then written on other thing,
full flame and all flame, steady and true;
a murmuring comfort, in sweetful all loving,
but yet the affirming in all that ever will;

grasping the palm of unmade forever,
in self and out self, and nowhere and allwhere,
sightful within, yet turning in overview.

All that is known in the past or the future
falls in a sunfold, slipping through cloud lanes;
all stories written, bound in the Maker,
cast in the play of the master and mind;
dimensionwise gloried and storied,
in colour change found and remembered;
produced from a thought wave, varied,
peopled, placed, by some miracle, heavenly signed.

From the One:
universes into bubbles bursting, breathless,
until the Spirit stirs among the star tracks;
willing to love, willing the love children
into life shape, many formed and far to wide;
all in his holding, safely for love's sake keeping,
within his grace fast and nurtured;
many creations from his begetting,
launched outwards
and in his outstretched arms,
new images found in love abide.

The One in his love is pain-wise, knowing birth
    pangs,
bearing for the full term, and beyond,
as he cares and loves so small, each atom

caught in his ever loving, and so many loves
    borne;
and yet, his love an infinity larger
than everything giving; in the dying breath
he loves and suffers, taking the children, flesh
    free,
into their spirit castles, home to eternity.

2
The Star Maker

The One
gives breath, a million years long lasting,
and then another sustaining, universe holding;
power into being glories,
webs of beauty soul weaving, matrix forming,
galaxies waiting, bursting with stars;
naked lights glowing, gases far swirling
into new spaces, the desert wastes filled
with turn and change growing;
the minute, the colossal, side by side exploding
into fragments, rock giants, as the time shell
     tears.

Everything that is, in the new dream opening,
filling with events, choices to mind as
whirlwinds of thinking dervish space limits,
then turn back again to the heart pulsing veins;
chaos upflurries through the not yet marches,
and words call to order
primeval forces,
locked in the hub of dark hurricanes.

Galaxies splitting,
cones and twists swirling,
turning on axles, brute hammered with gold;
all guiding lights flaring,
Newton lines, Einstein curves thrusting
equation to system unfurling,
laws settling pattern wise;
the One, his maker hand waving
across circles wound, and there now, living
     sculpture,
a universe formed in the gleam of his eyes.

A galaxy corner, still steaming,
hot cloud balls yet spinning,
and debris out flung;
but holds it all gathered,
side slipping out of each motherful sun;
molten lumps cooled, and hardening well
into space rolling marbles,
a gigantic game of time bagatelle;
and the star squadrons, look!
– now weaving their newly spun spell.

Spheres split, swerve veering on,
while birth giving to moons
all silky and light shimmering there,
like mirrors for god children;
and Saturn
with glittering ring, swinging diamond fire

on fast, invisible strings outswung;
while over the orbit lines
hurtle sundered, living hot coals
struck off like sparks,
raised in great arches of comet rushing,
far and away and swooping along.

One planet shines greenward to blue,
infant of moon light, lullaby near;
swamp steaming over, festooned with gas glow,
and under the mud gurgle
a festering, futuring to life heat;
commas and fullstops all wriggling forceful,
mingled in slime clots,
pairing to globules of glistening
where pulses of soul song struggle and beat.

Water and earth frames all bounded,
dragon backs of land free to the wind;
foam clad the oceans,
leviathan waves pound pummelling,
masses of seaway heap hurling,
cloud spirals jostling, up whirling;
and then the shivering and settling,
as snow peaks and sea caverns form;
sun bars watery pale, just peering
into the dusk dark
of the rough ready, rollicking storm.

Thunder in heaven struck barrages
crashes steepway to valley,
and monotonous hail flings
a thousand years lasting;
rip river cutting, cliff hanging falls,
and between the riot runs of rain
root stripes all quiet and growing;
and steam stirring in squirming pools
swim the billions and trillions of snailtips
that struggle to multiply,
link locking again and again.

The word whispers, ages echoing,
time and space ordering,
atom whorls milled
into shapes and forms of living flesh;
and from the ocean edges
tiny buttons of life,
capture fringes of swampy land,
chewing the algae,
serrating providential sedges.

3
The Dream Maker

Tiny fishes spurting, slick darting
and corals, island castle building
pink and purple deep,
and worms and jelly fish mud mooching,
as if they had eternity to search;
small bubbles of life
gleam touched with brush wands
of blue and gold and green and white;
some miracle, tinting scales and fins
until the flashing shoals
are rainbow stippled,
all marble splashed and treasure bright.

And so time softly drift layers
a thousand million years dreamwise,
God thinking each space hour
from his aching never sleep;
watching atom flows, steady waiting
his potent chemistry;
now and again over toppling
mountain and sea hold;
rough hewing islands from seabeds,

dipping horizon below ocean,
stir brewing mix and lather of mould.

Tumbling soil simmers with seed rippling,
all swelling and birth bursting,
ferns and pine pyramids
thrusting so small, then up the wide sky scaling,
on hills spreading dark with wild forest fold;
cumbersome great insects, with wax vivid wings,
far strumming and droning
their noon hot long sorties
through archways of joy green
and glint glittering sun prints of gold.

Sea witches thrive, dive long and swooping
among the uncountable, shivering shoals;
one generation to next on growing
they change and they range, strong striving,
off shedding their outlived scaly skins;
and glorious and grand, the spout leaping whales
gather and gambol in crowds, undisturbed;
and there the cavern mouthed sharks,
at dashing and thrashing speeds,
shadow dance deep down
among fantastical traceries of weeds.

And so all fresh beauty burgeons
in flesh and flower new opening,
multiplying, searching formations,

mysterious, atoms in geometry counted,
    patterned;
another hundred million years on going
dreaming a thousand Edens far away from;
leaving old fossil puzzles
to tease fill posterity's daydreams,
and history lines to count and enquire
the generations of mysterious rock runes;
all light years before the mind tread
could think through the boundaries and paths
of earth field and heavenly shire.

First the land eager reptiles
flip flapping untried the shore edge,
gasping, slide kicking,
and heaving this strange breath to being;
staying a brave, a fearful death panic,
then slipping back to safe and home surface;
whiskering out yet again, with throat muscle
    moans,
more head up and dare devil,
snuffling new, tongue tickling morsels,
nose testing the land breeze,
sun sampling glorious moments
upon smooth sea patterned stones.

Another
plateau of time turns to fast climb;
a living space change up turning

as land easy creatures all scramble
to nest eager young on the beach fall;
risking the living up air levels;
brisk splitting millions of seeds
to make a landful of life shapes;
galloping twenty ton monsters by the uncount
roaming the fern feathered plains;
and dizzying dare fresh the heights
those hosts of curious tree sitters;
while below, ploughing deep in the soil crumble
scavenging, and creep cutting,
legions of joint curling centipedes.

Air beating and useless
for aeons and aeons akimbo flapping,
old fishy fins devise then a land change,
a growth into flailing, crazy wing tips;
up there the clumsy,
spread shadowing dragons flutter
way above the psychedelic mothflies.
Swooping from an awesome sky, dive devil,
with ghoulish, terrifying screams,
the hunting pterodactyls clutch at
tiny, scurrying lizards
and claw fat, wriggling elvers
from rock tumbling, gurgling streams.

And then once again
unleashed fireworks rush, all swoop flaming,

meteors sizzling their hot wind glow,
and comets wild through flash flying;
the earth ball multi-bombarded,
craggy lumps of metal crash mauling;
then the mega bang flipping
the death's angel time bomb;
all crack shattering with world shake
and smoking the suffocating air;
strangling the lanky dinosaur tribes
to heaps of wrinkling flesh flow,
storing their bones in the ashes –
giant puppets unstrung, all twist twirled,
and into the distance of history hurled.

Moulding his damp clay mind again,
the One turns in his meditating,
creating, generating
world premiere galleries of new fauna,
of kindred all kinds herding,
adaptive and muscle lined well;
lollopping, fur bundled kangaroos,
and scaly, snapdragon crocodiles;
ostriches, showy and royal feathered
and glistening hippo archipelagos;
turtles and snakes, hieroglyphic backed,
and apes, lope swinging with kingly ease
among sun dizzy, shade wrapping trees.

And then the ape adventurer stamps out,
upright and gravity balanced;
a scary, wondrous, hair prickling sight there,
power padding the leafy hung ways,
flexing his lump bulging arms,
beating his ribby proud chest drum
and shouting his joyful, ape hallelujahs;
and following
the shambling, ambling clever ape,
the one that sharpens river stones
to hammer open the coconuts,
all luscious and glistening inside,
and to shave the flesh off the rabbit legs
down to the crunchy white bones.

The Maker ponders then,
the apeform and the future:
a larger brain to foster
a slick computer box, a mind holder
to solve complex equations;
the potent risks devil made, fanning
a hundred mischief offspring,
spark flamed to evil.
But the great heart of loving
imagines an ape his image growing,
a creature formed in beauty, truth wise;
free as the air to roam the starry tracks,
one with judgement, reason guided,
rendering good for good,
creator ape with power to match.

The Maker dream fashions
an assembly line in mind moulds,
a hundred thousand years trying;
ape working hand magic,
but reason only glimmering;
another digging log to sail
for exploring gleaming otter ways;
ape scraping accidental flame,
burning rabbit morsels;
inventing colour stains for wall symbols,
starting an art trend;
learning with fired mudblocks
the new home nesting ways;
round the door gap planting
wild strawberry tastes and bread oats;
hunter ape, spear and arrow fanged
stealing wolf skins for wife coats –
the human seeds sowing, growing,
thoughts source become
into aching dreams of their own,
folly and wisdom stuffed together
in finely sculptured
envelopes of human flesh and bone.

4
Breasting the Sunlight

The all life is, reveals himself, unshutters
 light,
flickers soulwise, moment to moment,
eye gleam in twist and sweep of stars turning;
a miracle Homer sung and remembered,
ever echo in mind, in glaze and daze of dawn
 glow;
an Earth, forge blasted in heaven borne flame,
hammer blows of words working,
the vision stripped to beauty, cast well,
eternal dream made, gossamer blown into time.

A yard of earth spaced, opened to birth chance,
the now in the tick of time gloried,
stretched to a life span;
pulsing a round through season and season,
stare standing down all coloured days,
wonder bursting the sense lines;
breasting the sunlight
that owns and rules, spins every flower,
dazzles and warms in the mothering
upon the rolling, cloud gathered ways.

There still and waiting, wake filled,
a curve around the clock,
new again miracle of night burgeons;
myriads of morsing stars
in sparkle fountains falling through dark blue
    deeps;
on dappled clouds
moon slip unmoored, slow drifting there;
far to sail, dove feathered, all soft silvered the
    waves,
as if to tell of all dreams true found,
worth seeking, always, yes always, heaven aware.

Constantly new phased,
miracle of mystery in dusk and dawn turning;
end and beginning saintly hallowed
as days and nights trail
in glorious light edge neverending;
benedictions over twilight curtains falling,
as the Earth boom swings over the hill, to sweep
ever eastwards towards breaking resurrection,
bearing light for long hoping
to the aching dark;
and far round the arc
another horizon with red streamers flying,
the same sun dipping westerly
into the quiet womb, soul fostering,
wave rocking, half human angels to sleep.

Tight corded, life bound and mouth open
to the mother sun,
cliff angled to light and shade,
the earth, bead small in the universe,
whirligig, dipping and lifting
on the lilt of the star destined path;
oceans and continents stirring,
swaying the rhythms of nature's song given;
textures never still, seasons splashing,
stippled collages of colour
across the curve of sweet earth unfurled;
patch of land, bowl of water, all full there,
thrive getting, love swarming endlessly;
economy of atoms patterned, shaped and
     nurtured,
an enchantment of striving,
through the heart of a buzz busy world.

Bitter breath snows, waste upon waste layered,
long turning the generation folds,
deeply at each pole sleeping,
where wild hurricanes stretch, far outreaching,
curling the ice freshened air up bankwise
and way through the cloud lines;
spinning curve current, and then down dome,
Africa bound, round to the rock desert wastes
where heat hovers heavily, death still
over each wavering dune;
but then soft air breath rising,

dreamily steady as it goes;
hungry vulture wings soar lifting;
and black glinting eyes searching,
seeking, scraps of flesh on bone
roasting on some oven hot slab
of sun whitened stone.

In another place,
a quarter globe across the next horizon's mist,
surge rolling mile on mile of townless plain,
where slow winds wind and whisper
through gold warm seas of corn;
and then a boil brew of storm
all thunderous and rip tearing, full wild riding
each running wave leaping
down the burst flowing Mississippi vein;
breaking all bounds, shock carrying
broken car and shaken shackdown to the mother
      sea;
while over the ocean eastwards and dull grey,
new leaping gales take up the roving song
and wash the tentacle rocks of Europe
with their smoking salt tang spray.

The wind sings down the Indus
boisterous and chase chevying,
monsoon whirling rope rains,
slap whipping up jungle slopes;
the back lash spreading southwards

lambasting oceans far and long
where frantic chariot leaping foam waves
rear and roar around the world
with unleashed power, thrust bearing on.
Another offspring wind
snorts marrow chilling gusts that wheeze
among the island coasts
which then fade to a whispering
in the vineyards round the lilac waters
of the sleep laden Tyrrhenian seas.

Section Two

THE FOUNTAIN OF LOVE

Prologue

The new born baby cries,
    longing for,
    longing for the breast,
        the love bending breast.

Out of the fountain bursting
    its life has come,
        looking for,
        looking for the surge of love,
        the love swollen tide
        its quest.

Love is the ocean swirling,
    within the new life urging
        to follow the gleaming pathway,
        seaway to the west
        way to the west.

And that love is the heart beat,
    the throb of the endless universe,
    from the veins of God flowing,
        flowing to all that is,
        that is,
        in the star scatter of spring.

Time is an eternal ring,
    turning, turning,
    and space is an infinite fire,
    burning, burning,
        as the phoenixes sing,
        as they wing
        from flame to flame,
        as they wing.

And God said and he keeps on saying,
    let there be,
    let there be life
    and let there be death;
    let there be love
    as the thrushes sweetly sing
        in the woodland glade,
        as they sweetly sing.

There is a shore beyond the waves,
    a far distant shore,
    and forlorn
    the seagulls cry, and cry;
        echoing,
        the seagulls cry.

But beyond that shore is another sea
    stretching to eternity
    where waves wander endlessly;
    and there all love is singing,

winging over wave,
over wave winging;
as the wind's voices sigh,
voices sigh.

Still each newborn child is bound
to love and others loving,
as the brave soul goes roving
over the universe,
from one sky
to another sky,
starry sky.

The fountain of love is flowing,
ever flowing;
and all those loves are blessed,
and every living thing
is blessed.
To be born and to die
in the fountain of love
is never to die,
never to die.

1
The Petals of the Rose

Ten thousand joys of living spring into life
    and their dancing glories spin,
    into the universe crowding,
    crowding into time,
        and filling all space,
        all space filling,
        with boundless gifts of grace.

Energy bounds from those suns
    that whirl within the galaxies,
    and the galaxies twist
    and thrust their tentacles
        into the dust,
        the golden dust,
        that forms
        light years of shining ways.

To race along those starry paths
    is like a heaven unfolding,
    unfolding in the mind,
    the mind's eye where dreams are born;
        but this is no dream,

    expanding from the womb
    to fill so many days.

There are beings, countless beings,
  bursting from the living fountain;
  and all heavens and all earths are filled
  with the glory of shapes and colours,
    and symphonies,
    and words of love forming
    to praise the source of all
    that from the fountain falls.

And down the many walls of stars they run,
  angels and men,
  myriads, myriads,
  of angels and men;
  they shout at the glory and they sing
    in the rivers of light
    where the opening clouds
    reveal far, spacious halls.

They find the rainbow and the moon
  and catch the petals of the rose;
  upon the hills they see
  the glint of sun at dawn
  through a window of mist,
  and on the ocean's rim they hear
    the breaker,
    the thunderous breaker

        as it rolls
        to the marram grass,
        where the sandpiper calls.

And on one world the seasons turn,
    turn from year to year,
    bringing the rain and snow,
    unfurling the wind;
        and the wind blows
        blows it all away,
        far and far away.

And on another world the patterns form
    as the sun rises and sets,
    and the four moons follow,
    night after night,
        gleaming with pale, blue light
        across a silent world
        where no eye yet sees,
        by night or by day.

And on another world the life teems,
    oceans and air and earth
    all filled with sense and stir;
    creatures in millions thrive
        in their elements
        and multiply themselves
        time and again,

        time and again,
        in the fountain's spray.

The fountain of love is flowing,
    ever flowing;
    as night follows each glorious day,
    and as the cool dew falls,
    all loves embrace;
        and to love
        in the fountain of love
        is never to die,
        never to die.

2
Straws Blowing in the Wind

For a time, one world is enough
for one world is infinite variety,
as the child becomes aware
of feeling and knowing,
of making and believing;
and life is a wonder,
a wonder indeed.

The tribes and races gather the fruit of their
wombs
and they baptize them with fire
in a world of wanting,
of wanting and desire;
and the rich flames glow,
a fountain of love in the veins,
and new streams flow,
all wanting freed.

And people become their wishes,
as wishes grow into actions

and they spark with fresh energy,
working and working and working,
    day and night working,
    in their ventures revelling,
    producing, making,
    as their wishes breed.

But spacious minds expand beyond
    the businesses of concrete and of steel;
pulsing thoughts light candles
which light more candles,
    while mirrors multiply the mysteries;
        gods grow in the mind
        as attempted explanations clarify
        those damned elusive questions –
    O why? O why? O why?

And as many answers came as came before
    to the last generation of questions,
    so many answers to the riddles
    posed by the universe;
        and systems flicker like shadows
        as philosophers ponder
        in their caves.
        But are the systems death proof,
        and truth polished,
        as they spiral to the sky?

And the purists stick to numbers and symbols,
    finding their truth in small things,
    reliable truths in milligrams.
        If it can be measured,
        it is measured
        and carefully recorded,
        carefully recorded,
        as they weigh and quantify.

Some find their answers in the warp and weft of
        words
    as word crafting they ponder
    and play games with fictional truth;
    but is their truth any less true
    than the earth and the sky and the sea,
    than footprints in the wet sand?
        Words provide their own miracles,
        straws blowing in the wind.

There are those who glory in colours and shapes,
    shapes and colours folding and pressing
    into questions and answers unlimited;
    the face on the canvas smiles
    with more mystery than the face itself,
        and that is a consequence
        to be reckoned with;
        that art concealing art
        which compounds the question
        and puzzles the mind.

Who is there who can make sounds into miracles
    with air and metal,
    and wood and string?
      These are the Merlins of the air waves,
          the markers of intervals
          between the blackbird's song
          and the first streak of dawn,
          that few, very few, can find.

The fountain of love is flowing
      as the wind scatters seed after seed
      while the autumn evenings die;
      and these strange happenings are noted,
          noted in the diary of time.
          Is anything forgotten,
          as all that loves is blessed
          and is by eternity signed?

3
Scorching the Butterfly

One thing leads to another and from a sombre
     matrix
  disasters and delusions germinate and grow,
haunting the glories behind the scenes;
    as suffering breaks the spirit
    so despair fastens on hope,
    and new perspectives,
    blinkered by pain,
    limit tired dreams.

Who to blame is yet another question,
   for a godless world becomes reality,
    where poverty and riches, hunger and plenty,
     are poles that never meet;
     hate your neighbour as yourself
     is where temptation falls;
     and blind nature
     sourly plays
     its cruel themes.

A frightening game of consequences
    changes the rules, implicates innocence

  in tournaments where good and evil joust
    for winning or losing souls;
    the saint sings alleluia,
    but the sinner stops his ears
    and complains bitterly
    that no angel has spoken,
    that God is not what he seems.

The earthquake claims its victims equally,
  as rich and poor, saint and sinner,
  are crushed by falling beams;
  and so the godless sceptic thrives
  on his unanswerable questions.
    Who can prove his God?
    Let him write his formula
    in the dust from which he came
    and let the wind
    blow his words away.

The warring nations have their centenary fling
  and batter beauty with guns and bombs,
  scorching the butterfly with cinders.
  proud anthems roll to echoing drums
  as dying boys whimper in pain –
    again and again,
  as one generation follows another
    in the odour of decay.

The pimp collects his fees, night after night,
    as lovely bodies are carelessly soiled
    in a fantasy of loveless sweat;
    and at the rich end of the scale
        beauty is freely given
        for the same end –
        a stab in the dark,
        after the dance,
        with little delay.

Pestilences scour the world for victims
    and the infant dies without knowing
    the joy or the meaning of his days;
    for his counted hours
    are over before his senses can supply
        his opening world
        with clues to his existence,
        with names for what he sees.

Ideals crumble in the dark, uncertain valley
    and love is a memory of home
    which has been pulverized
    by the disappointments of empty weekends;
        treachery and faithlessness
        are familiar acquaintances
        and truth is a stranger
        in uncharted seas.

The drunk and the homeless squatter
    lie together under a bridge,
    dry at least in the storm;
    but morning has to come,
        and further wandering
           through the friendless streets
        of a teeming metropolis,
where haunting scents of coffee tease.

Contradictions multiply in the dawn
    and in the passing beams
    of the number eight 'bus
    a face smiles alight;
        and then the muddy grey
        of the wet pavements,
        where milling feet swish,
        takes over the mind
        in anonymous unease.

4
The Angel Stairs

Yet somewhere deep in the ice closed mind
   there is a word of sense, a grace of sorts,
   a flower in bud that bids for light;
   towards that distant gleam
   it strives for its purpose,
      from Arctic night
      aching for the warmth of spring.

Is it a revelation – or an impulse bred
   in cells of ancestral testament?
   Whatever be the impetus of sanity
   that stretches from the swamp of death,
   the life it beckons to is worth
      a dream or so,
      a vision hopeful on the wing.

Like a mountain higher than a thought,
   the days ahead stretch to new horizons;
      and more new horizons;
   and it is hard to keep a heaven ahead
   of the hell that unfolded yesterday;
   but the thrust of crocuses

  is stronger than the snow bound soil,
    as they spike green
    from their lengthy wintering.

But heaven is there in that hopeful dream
  and upwards is not a bad description,
  for it is hard to climb the angel stairs
    that Jacob dreamt about;
    though messengers have come
    from time to time
    to tell the tale
    of the pilgrimage.

To dream in gaol of that tortuous progress
  was difficult for a tinker once,
    but he persevered
  and his message was heard,
    clearly heard,
  by many in the valley bottom
    as they waited for a guide,
    a prophet or a sage.

The name of the destination was revealed
  a long time ago, to a king;
  and many a poet wrote on the subject,
  swearing to fight for truth for truth and
    beauty,
  to follow the holy child,
  to love, to care, to die

        for the sake of those journeying
        through this passing age.

To mount the ladder that leads to grace
    is to reach for the hand of Christ;
    and salvation from the abyss
    awaits the faithful pilgrim
    as he scrambles rung by rung,
        stair by painful stair,
        to the promised stars,
        uncertainly aware.

Aware of the motion of the universe
    as it spins round the point of thought,
    the eternal word of God
    the speech of wind and fire;
    aware of voices all around,
        the spirit guiding
        through the twilight days,
        and nights awake with care.

Knowing the inward truth in part
    and puzzling the larger truth
    in moments of singular clarity,
    the answers to all the questions —
    the who, the what and the where —
    which underpins the canopy

   that limits vision;
   the endless questions
   that lay the wires bare.

And so the dream on open wing
  attempts the truth, attempts the crossing
  of the corruscating ocean;
  and so the shuttered cage
  becomes a place for journeying
   beyond the do not dare
   of daily words of caution,
   and the dream expands,
   way through
   the golden morning air.

5
The Soul Healers

And a vision comes to certain individuals
   selected by the final powers that be;
   these few can feel the current of the Spirit
   flowing in their very veins,
   and angel voices call across the void
   that lies between this earth
       and some far heaven,
       angel voices,
       there and here.

New revelations make the stars shine bright
   and songs of praise resound in every dawn;
   alleluias cry across the street
   as the sun shafts, gleaming on windows
       in no ordinary way —
       yet normal as each day,
       for each day the beauty falls
       in a rainbow filled tear.

God is with us in the chorus of the early light
   and God is there upon the cloud,
   the cloud that shutters mystery

across the rose garden
petalling down the heaven breeze,
   glorying in the sky paths,
   and chanting down the air streams,
   the Jesus bells
   crystal and clear.

The soul healers march together across the
      universe,
   the people of the revelation,
   borrowing the tongues of angels,
   the miracle wands of Merlin;
      and the far flung folk half lost
      listen for the speech of fire
      that breaks from the valley folds.

Alleluia is the song of the faithful,
    the dreamers of the silver lining,
    those who feather through the storms
    and quiet the seas, the surging seas
      that pound on the rocks
      of the shaking continents,
      as the Spirit holds,
      all in his hand holds.

Glory calls from the hillside meadows,
   where the sheep bells tinkle gently,
   gently falling to the gurgling stream
      which flows to the ocean,

   flows endlessly to the ocean,
   where God holds each drop of rain
   until the sun shower
   opens the marigolds.

The ageing are ageless in the mind and spirit
  as they approach the homeward slopes,
  just over the watershed;
  they feel no different
  as the years gather and multiply,
    as the body aches and fumbles —
   for the glory is within,
   a deathless, living word.

The rainbow and all beauty are still in the eye
  and the music of the seasons is joyous
  for the hope of the strong,
  the faith of the true;
    God is with them always
   as they walk down the valleys
   of the land of promise
   where the tongue of prophecy
   is even now heard.

Glory to the Father and to the Son
  and to the Holy Spirit,
  the Lord of all creation;
  in the night he grasps the soul
  and touches it with his grace,

and in the day he brings flame
    as to the hearth of heaven
    where love s fire is stirred.

And the song of the blackbird is echoing clear
    through the summer woodland,
    where the light and shade of youth
    are green in recalling;
        for age and youth are one
        in the dream of passing years,
        in the tally of tales untold,
        as the flicker of life to death
        is quietly fringed and blurred.

6
Grace Upon Grace

And out of the fountain of love in glorious
    spate,
  the endless works of God and man
  go on and on, eternally on,
  as words and colours and sounds are made,
  patterns forming in the wind,
  beauty in the trickling sand dune;
    away, away to the ocean,
    the boundless ocean,
    the miracles and marvels flow.

A man sits down in his evenings
    and conjures a sonnet of his thoughts,
    and then he opens his heart to love
    taking his woman by the hand
    to give her his universe of words;
    and she unfolds her breasts
      to the child they have made
      in the heat of a moment,
      a season ago.

The Spirit walks with the summer morning
    across the grey hills and the green valleys
    where the hawthorn boughs splash foam
    along the meadows and lanes;
    the shadows yet dark in the woodland
    as the young rabbits scamper
        to the dewy banks of the river —
        God revealing his glory
        for all to know.

The woman spends her hours moulding red clay
    and she spins it into a vase
    of wonderful and satisfying shape;
    her man chooses from the flowers of the
        field
    and gives them to her,
    embracing her love with his,
        as they watch,
        watch the seasons go by.

The Spirit walks on the water across the lake
    as the wind ruffles the surface,
    reflecting a thousand sun darts;
    there the dazzling kingfisher swoops
    to take the silver, wriggling fish,
        while the shoals pass below
        quiet and unaware
        under their rippling sky.

The child takes his crayons and scribbles,
    trying to catch some sign of meaning
    in his world of magic;
    the shapes whirl through his hands
        in self explanations
        and the innocent joy of infancy
        flashes bright in his eye.

The Spirit meditates in the scorching desert lands
    where few things grow and little moves
    as the sun stands at noon;
    for ever, it seems, the heat descends
    like a lifeless blanket
        over the rocks and canyons,
        and silence empties all space.

Crowds of people gather round the gnarled stones
    which have leaned there for several ages;
    they make music and dance
    and they sing their dark liturgies,
    attempting to pierce the mystery
        of the lights in the heaven,
        as they take hold of eternity
        and scrutinize its face.

The Spirit glories through the forest lands
    where the flowers dazzle even more
    than the cackling birds;
    scattered sun blotches

    pierce the green roof
    and glisten on gaudy wings
    which ruffle the lianas
    in the joy
    of the courting chase.

The fountain of love is flowing free
  across the continents and islands,
  over the oceans and seas,
  arching high
  and swooping low
    through the soul of the universe,
    love following love,
      grace upon grace.

7
Centre of Flame

The old cathedral climbs above the dreaming
    square,
  where on worn cobbles of ancient vintage,
  feet have ached to the tombs of saints;
  and in the shadowy nave,
  splashed with purple and red,
  crumbling features of stone act out
     the decaying legends
     of space and time
     under the arching choir.

The ancestors of the Gothic architects
    rode cautiously through the forests,
    wary of the holy presences,
    clutching their charms;
    but sword in hand,
    they took the rich green land
      and sowed their children
      in flame and fire.

The bells echo across the fields and woods,
    telling their tales of festival and song

in places where holy men have spoken words
to the very angels in heaven;
the bells mark the months and years
across the dark furrows of history
and give tokens of faithfulness
    to the generations as they pass,
      pass beneath the signpost spire.

Old folk gather round the stone cross of Christ,
    planted long ago in the village square,
    and they remember their dead,
    carved like carcasses in old wars.
    The children play round the tombs,
        calling to the morning
        as it passes through their bodies,
    the dawn shining in their eyes.

The holy presence awaits in the church,
    gathers around the church,
    as the Sundays trundle along,
    like slow trains to eternity;
    and the holiness grows
    as if the prayers of many pilgrims
        filled the stones and slates
        with pensive sighs.

Invisible saints map their thoughts
    round each village and town,
    and pray silently for the living,

for every hasty soul;
and guardian angels hold
each precious candle
    that burns in the window
    of each body bound home,
    as the years pass swiftly by.

An unkempt man sits alone in the desert,
    incongruously perched on a pole;
    he tests the iron in his burning soul
    and searches for God in the distances,
    as well as in the well of his soul;
    impervious to heat and cold,
        his thoughts gather around
        his future death.

Upon the crags and peaks of red mountains
    on a planet where no foot has trod,
    the holiness of God
    waits in the depth of his love
    for the first life to move;
        time is quite still, as if
        the days and nights were one,
        and only the wind stirs
        the dust with hot breath.

In a heart of light in a far galaxy
    the thought of a mystery ponders
    the indelible seed of life;

      and the seed bursts into flower
      as if the first soul were born.
          This is the beginning
          without any end,
          the holy centre of flame
          in its transparent sheath.

The holiness hurts in its conception,
     like love without lust burning
     in a chalice of pure thought;
     this is the not born that never dies,
     in its eternal simplicity,
         the gleam of hope
         to the eye of faith.

8
The Cloud of Beauty

The fountain of love is also the fountain of
 truth
 as the light flickers across the universe;
 the possibility of untruth is there
 and the choice is there, to mouth a lie,
 or to stand in the light
 where all can see the naked flame,
  the soul behind the eye,
  where truth is sown.

The seekers look for the ultimate decoder
 and in their seeking find themselves,
 grasp the reflection of an idea
 that seems to pierce a veil,
 as if the image was the fact;
 but they see only an edge
  of the polished stone of destiny,
  the shining crystal corner
  behind the dark unknown.

All the wise and great of countless centuries
 have only sensed the meaning of their

>   several years,
> for they see only a segment
> of eternity's vast ring,
> a mere centimetre
> of infinity's unmeasured skein;
> > but the glory of the vision
> > falls like the rainbow's arch
> > when the thunder shower
> > sweeps down.

The cloud of beauty catches red and gold
> and through the tracery of light and shade
> there echoes the thrill of a thrush's song;
> a joy and a delight are found
> around the image of sound and shape;
> > and from the magic matrix
> > that dreams our world alive
> > the wonder stirs within.

What are the millions of permutations
> that trim the light years of our space and
> > time?
> – the atoms that make the primrose bloom,
> the intervals that open out
> the dawn with songs of praise?
> What are the scents of wind and tide,
> > the tang of salt and sea,
> > the warmth of sun on skin?

This beauty falls across the aching mind
    like painted leaves upon the autumn frost;
    the eyes, the lips, the breasts of woman
    and the angled structures of a man
    open the gates of heaven –
    though these too become
        like leaves upon the ground,
        as the wind blows chill
        in the teeth of winter's grin.

The quiet saint kneels in his prayers and forms
    a glory around his mind, a holy good,
    a loving smile, a helping hand,
    though he does not know his saintliness;
    he holds the world in his thoughts
    and cares for it like a forlorn child,
        loving all with equal passion,
        trading himself for souls.

The gaudy prostitute is good at heart
    and helps the needful when she can;
    her tawdry trade cannot despoil
    the gentle mothering she brings
    to the blind beggar
    and the crippled child;
        she will not be forgotten
        in the heavenly scrolls.

The nun fingers her rosary whenever time
    releases her from love and care,
    from the human flotsam in the city gutter,
    the dying dregs, forgotten
    as the selfish, hasty world goes by;
        her eyes reflect her God,
        and the dawn her love,
        as the chapel bell tolls.

The millionaire the church publicly disowns
    ponders on the tiny needle's eye
    and the proportions of the proverbial camel,
    as he makes his soaps and perfumes
    to scent the satin skin
    of duchesses and whores;
        but he has his saintly moments,
        unknown to the world,
        as he tops to the brim
        a million begging bowls.

9
A Few Worthwhile thoughts

Jesus took a pebble and threw it far,
far into the future, and the ripples
are still circling round a doubtful world;
but the love and the pain are still there
in the next man and in the next woman,
    just as he painted them.
    a portrait of the divine,
    incarnate in him.

Socrates was on the same wave length, of course,
    and he gave himself to the jealousy and the
        hate
of the next man and the next woman;
he told us the truth in his walking
around the courtyards of philosophy,
    and he guessed at the true God
    in his probing
    of the universe's rim.

Gotama told the next man and the next woman
    the same kind of message of love,

and he penetrated the eye of God
without seeing the face of the One;
    but he was a luminary
    in a dark, dark world,
    and his words are good
    when the lamp is dim.

Russell was a great guy with a big, big heart
    and he loved and he cared like a saint,
    though to the true meaning of life
    he was congenitally blind;
    no doubt he is still philosophizing
        about the new life he now has
        in the dispensation of Christ –
    after a stunned rebirth.

Muhammad was a dreamer in the desert places,
    but his words echo round the mosques
        ceaselessly;
    his vision was like the noonday sun,
    hard hitting on the burning rock;
    and the lines of good and evil
        he drew like rectangles
        so that no misunderstanding
        prevents a man from knowing
        what life is worth.

Lao-Tse left a few worthwhile thoughts behind,
    after perusing vast, inscrutable plains;

  he found life was very good
  and saw that the God of all
  is in the forest and the lake,
    on the mountain and in the sky;
  he knew that there is
  only a fine difference
  between sadness and mirth.

Thomas More expressed his gallant soul with style
  and even joked himself towards his death,
  as if he knew he was within his rights
  and would receive an invitation to the final
    feast;
  he gave his life to God and gave up all,
  his family and friends, all dear to him,
  because he could not varnish truth,
    because he would not compromise.

Dante had a splendid vision of the universe
  and of both views beyond the grave;
  he frightened many into churches
  and others out of them,
  because he made his dream so real –
    as vivid as a glass of wine
    and crucial as a crust of bread
    when a beggar starves and dies.

Handel brought his dreams to noble sound
  and caught the hearts of those with faith,

as well as many who teetered on the edge;
his choruses are great converters
to the cause of Christ,
and in his oratorios he lives
 as long as men can last
 within their prayers
 and Godly sighs.

Darwin was a merchant of cold water,
 but he sought the truth with dedication,
as history challenged him,
because he wanted system;
and he showed mankind
that the lines of evolution
 carry the genes onward
 across the continents,
 across the starry skies
 from universe to universe
 onward driving.

10
To Rent for Joy

All that is belongs to undivided being,
    bound in flesh and thought for ever,
    dying to birth and being born to death;
    there is no end to the fountain of love,
    for it spumes out eternally and the love
        returns to whence it came;
            the One is in all being
            but he is himself unbound.

There is a ring of love that stretches
    throughout the galaxies and yet farther,
    and all are in communion
    with the God of grace and life,
    the living God who makes
    the blood pulse and the breath take,
        the joyfulness and the heart ache
        that makes the world spin round.

All species and races are his to make,
    to unmake and to bind with flesh,
    to fill with self and thought;
    all creatures mingle in the Godhead

and glory in their elements
of air and earth and water;
 the universe is theirs,
 and theirs to share
 with all who live,
 who are like kings uncrowned.

Praise to the Creator echoes around the universe,
 praise to the One from whom all beings
  come,
 praise from the far flung galaxies
and praise from the start of time;
 all space is his to own
 and ours to rent for joy,
 and through all light years
 token candles burn.

All belong to one another and all
 are loved like new born babies
 who have all space and time to play;
like leaves on a single tree
all human life is one;
 from the root, from the sap,
 the growing leaves still come
 as the years age and turn.

All minds are one in his, the One, the God
 who thinks upon his timeless, spanless
  Word,

with his love touching all awareness,
all that his thought has toiled
   into endless being;
   and his gracious giving of self
   has made selves freely,
   endowed to aspire and yearn.

A man and a woman take up their lives together
   and their love grows like blossom on the
      bough
   as their spring comes to summer;
   and their children join their love
   to stand in the circle of fire
   that holds their world for a while;
      a community of loving
      warming their hands.

But God himself is the ring of flame that throws
   each explosive spark of life into being;
   as the Father makes the earth into flesh,
   so the Spirit breathes on all that is,
   and the Son places his arms
   around the many races
      that teem over measureless seas
      into many sprawling lands.

All are filled with the love of God,
   the vibrating strings of many hearts
   that long for each other in the night

and wait for their love to fruit;
for the world is a tale of wonder
    where the wishing spills over
    and divides itself
      into many patterned strands.

And the fountain of love flows for ever
    as all wait for the sight and sound
    of the One whose loves are all loving;
    and even the unloved soon learns
    that his loving belongs to all,
    for his heart is beating with ours
      in the mighty heart of God,
      as the waters sweep over far sands
      to the everlasting shore.

Section Three

THE TAPESTRY

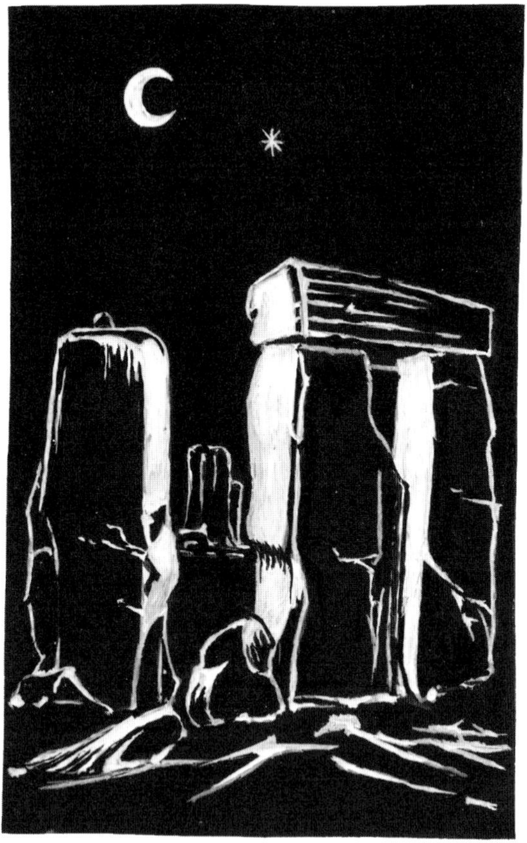

At Ashness Bridge

Under the bridge's old bent back
cool waters rush and gurgle down;
in fleece and foam they eddy and tack
along broad steps of smooth grey stone.

Over a blue and white barred sky
a skylark's song is lightly spun;
its glinting wing deceives the eye
and out of sight its course is run.

Across the fells cloud shadows move,
their beauty caught like fading dreams;
and bleak, grey crags tower above
the Derwent, where bright silver gleams.

Dark islands patch the tranquil lake
where saints long gone found peace of mind;
slow ripples on those green shores break
and leave this aching world behind.

The Thames at Abingdom

Reflected where the placid waters slowly
    pass,
pale yellow clouds paint an impressionistic sky;
the church's steeple stirs, quivers across smooth
    glass
as lazily the Thames goes drifting, winding by.

Then, brightly coated launches plough their
    steady ways,
breaking the quiet pools with eager, thrusting
    prows.
Along lush, waving meadows, where polished
    Friesians graze,
the fishermen disperse among low arching
    boughs.

From Cotswold pond and spring the waters whirl
    and wend,
onward and onward flowing to the distant sea;
like time the river moves towards its destined end,
in the deep ocean gulf of vast eternity.

Stonehenge

A strange voice through an archway softly
    sings
the secret of three thousand years fast sealed;
the crowding shadows gather in the wings
to watch the rites that hallow house and field.

Midsummer's anxious dawn is gasped and
    breathed:
the sun's ray flickers on the bloodstained stone.
The shining sacrificial sword unsheathed,
the druids wait, their savage psalms intone.

Across the misty plain bright sun birds fly,
dispelling dreams; a ring of silent runes
is left, enfolding realms of mystery,
through which the rising sun communes.

Wordsworth and Coleridge in the Quantocks

Through wood and field they rambled free as clouds,
scanning the distant Severn's lilac verge;
they found an Eden, far from city crowds,
truth meeting beauty where earth and heaven merge.

Past lonely farms, across long heather moors,
conducting the tune of every brook and spring,
their spirits soared in dizzy metaphors,
and here they touched the heart, the soul of everything.

The Quarry

The quarry cuts the hill away
as commerce makes its grim demand;
so beauty turns to stone and clay
where monsters eat the growing land.

The houses on the other side
are less than what they were last year;
the view is slashed – for gaping wide
the earth reveals a deep dark tear.

But where they dug two years ago
the lichens and the mosses spread;
new greenery begins to show
where once the jagged rocks seemed dead.

And as a thousand years pass by
the valley will reclaim its own;
for even towns one day will die
but trees will still be rooting down.

Swallows Beside the Bridge

The swallows swoop, loop, curve with verve,
along the water's edge they swerve,
a breath above the surface dipping
and through the bridge like arrows slipping.

And then up sky they soar in chase,
one to one bound, at breathless pace,
with easy grace, tracing rings
across the clouds, with touching wings.

Then flicking down, each dancing pair
back to the archway drawn, to dare
a feat of flight and not to flinch,
to miss the stonework by an inch.

Kingfisher

Beneath the heavy chestnut bough
the lone kingfisher flirts, a slip
of blue and gold across the slow
river's dark pool. A sudden dip

and the bright arrow dives, at home
in water. Like the fish it seeks;
a flurry as the foam and comb
of feathers climbs, the knife of beak

holding a wriggling silver trout;
a rainbow flash, it streaks away,
far down the river's curve, and out
of sight, too fast for thought to stay.

St Richard's Bridge

The Ouse at twilight softly flows
towards the vast eternal sea;
the west horizon redly glows
as evening settles peacefully.

The swans sail silently in fleet,
along the silken shining stream;
and not a soul moves in the street
as on the bridge I stand and dream.

I think of this place long ago
and of the saints who walked this way;
and in my heart I surely know
that God is at the end of day.

Devil's Dyke

The eye dips suddenly to meet
the Devil's trench across the down,
where legend claims he found defeat
by powers of light he tried to drown.

And light now fills the massive cleft
as glory falls on hill and wold;
the sun's shaft shoots its warp and weft
in tapestry of green and gold.

The white tracks leave their ancient spoors
where history paused and then passed by;
and pathways stretch to distant moors
where time and space roll with the sky.

In the Bishop's Garden, Chichester

Open and full the roses bend,
their scent heavy upon the air;
and bees each waiting flower attend
their sleepy drone a foil to care.

Splashes of colour charm the eye
and peace falls freely down the hours;
for God delights in husbandry
and speaks to all the Bishop's flowers.

The Piper Tapestry, Chchester

In cross and woven flame,
in mystery of sun,
the tapestry unfolds –
our God in gold unspun.

Creation is signed word,
ciphered in space and time;
through glorious Gospel speech
Domesday begins to chime.

The Trinity is spread,
in skilful threads unwound;
and in each secret seal
God's covenant is unbound.

At the Roman Palace, Fishbourne

A trencher found the treasure lost
for centuries pronounced long dead;
the art of Rome of patient cost
is now by curious tourists read.

The winged boy on the dolphin rides
as if he mounted yesterday;
the ghost of Cogidubnus strides
as if he still held kingly sway.

An ocean washed up to the walls
where quinquiremes with white sails came;
scorning the foul Atlantic squalls
to bear the scorching Roman flame.

But destiny has its own will
and fire brought down that Roman might;
the palace flowered with flames until
it burned to ashes one long night.

Yet under ash and mounds of clay
the dolphin boy was well concealed;
he passed the years in secret play
until his beauty was revealed.

Evening Over the Downs

Above the downs the evening star
is walking by the crescent moon;
the darkening sky goes deep and far
as night bestows its gracious boon.

The purple edge of earth meets sky,
curving away towards the west;
the feathered clouds like soft doves lie
asleep within a peaceful nest.

Under the Bridges

I see the shaky outline of a willow fringe
and deeper, the trembling figments of half drawn
       trees;
and in the fractured glazing of a hollow sky
the bare necessities of hope in rags of cirrus.

My eyes are fastened to a moving sleep; the
       surface
of breaking images figured through by attitudes
that flit, refracted, across the floor of reality.
So the water vacillates under my bridges.

Easter

Old city towers in bright sun, lend gold
burnished with hope to future dreams;
Jerusalem of Blake unspent
where angels make stairways to God.

Choruses, bold and fearless, sound
from arch to arch of sorrow's road;
towards Golgotha humping pain
through one by one hours of despair.

Crossed on the wood, man calls to heaven,
forsaken, forsaken soul in hell;
among the golden towers he dies,
cursed by a thief as time unfolds

its flowers. Three days for them to bloom,
lilies beneath a million spires;
first Easter falls upon the world
waking, dawn's song bursting the dome.

Bread and Board

The Word becomes bread in my mouth;
I quaff the cup of his shared blood,
expanding my brief lexicon
in his death's mystery now said;

and always spoken where the folk,
remembering, replay their God.
The pieces of the story fit
together end and beginning;

bud on the vine becomes this flask
of burning sweetness in me swirled;
and love begetting love is crumbled
from the wheatfield's offering.

Vast crowds assemble by the cross,
in their old wondering renewed;
the last blown breath of the dead king
ripples to where they reap his host.

His crown is hallowed in the glass,
where saints of all colours keep watch
over his ritual death, as life
springs from the board, pulsing our days.

Section Four

TWO TRILOGIES

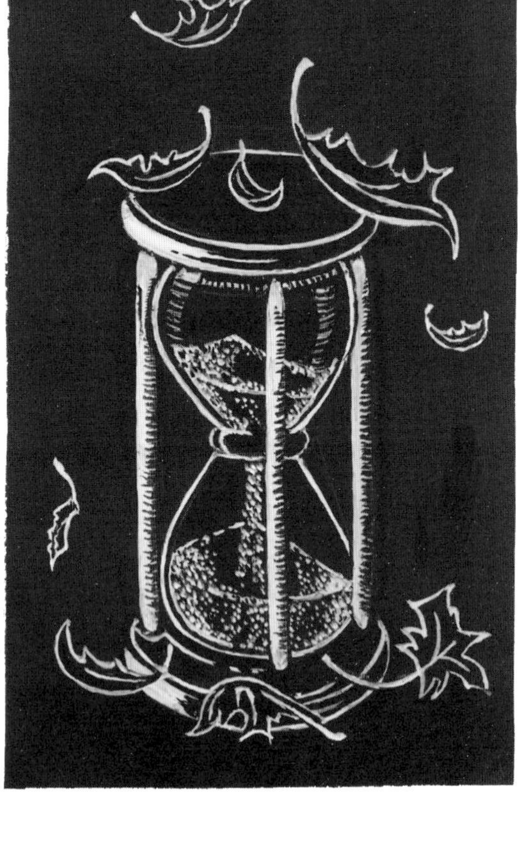

… *Three Love Poems*

1
I long to walk with you

At dusk, when first lone stars begin to spark,
I long for you to touch, to kiss to hold;
I long to lie beside you, thinking close
together, lost in day meeting the dark;
and then, as rising waves of love unfold,
to be the centre of your opening rose.

At dawn, after the warmth of sleep's embrace,
I long to walk with you in rain and sun;
I long to read to you Shelley and Keats,
to know with you their harmony and grace,
to dream of lovers gone, by time outrun,
to live our joy while time, our foe, retreats.

I long for you, my love, in heart felt prayer,
and till you come, I am but half aware.

2
Constant love

We saw a rainbow once, far on a hill,
God's wondrous art in gracious beauty bound;
your smile is in that rainbow's curve and gleam,
and when I think of you I see it still;
for in its beauty and in yours are wound
a mystery that fills my every dream.

Why is it that your every inch and line
bring images that time cannot remove?
Beauty it is indeed that charms my eye
but in that beauty lies a secret sign,
a power that burns within our aching love,
that marks the moving hand of destiny.

That rainbow speaks our promise to be true:
in constancy our path we shall pursue.

3
Love's old song

I hear a blackbird in the garden now,
and I remember when we woke at four
and heard a blackbird's innocent song's art;
it was as if my own voice sang to vow
my love for you; and could I love you more
I would, but love already brims my heart.

I wish you were beside me as I muse
on love's old song: the music you reveal
is not in string or pipe, though surely it fills
the air I breathe, flows in the streams that fuse
my very being into one, touches the seal
that forges my soul to what love wills.

Truly, my love, heaven is love that's free,
and love's song beggars all philosophy.

Three Autumn Poems

1
Love's season

Autumn again, the river's eaves
with surge of tawny floods beset;
paths in the park drifted with leaves
and shaggy verges dripping wet.

My fibres long for spring to come,
but how can autumn young love learn,
when thoughts of winter make love numb
and seasons in firm order turn?

Age cannot loose what time has bound
and must agree that spring has gone;
but love belies the season's round
and thought ignores the aching bone.

That spring of love thrusts through me now,
despite the outward autumn dream;
the buds are bursting on the bough
and sunshine glints upon the stream.

2
Late afternoon in October

Ice wind scatters the last rites of summer
as the old man sweeps in vain,
attempting to check the racing leaves,
years leaping beyond his grasp.
He lights a fire to burn the debris,
but still the wind blows
and sparks scatter across the lawns,
dreams he used to have.
The rain comes and spits in the blaze,
contemptuous of all he's done.
He swears quietly and takes
his barrow, brush and shovel
over to the shelter for a while,
hoping for some emcouragement.
But no light comes.
Wind and rain blur his landscape,
obliterating what was clear in youth.
Darkness falls and he makes for home,
his day a disappointment.
Supper is a last sacrament,
alone in his silent house.

3
November 1st

Autumn's blood slows down within my
    thoughts
until I feel the winter bite, cold to the core.
I wonder why, why the turning year,
why the painful twist and why, mysteriously
that winter gate extends across my path.
The question freezes on my lips almost,
but then, I think of nature's art,
the spring to follow, the world revolving
round eternal light – my God!
That should be true, should be –
for all this summer I have toiled
and now the grain is cut, the barn
filled with the produce of my years:
little enough.
But spring has always come,
so why not hope, green against the snow?
Rumours have said it would be so,
a year burgeoning from root to leaf,
beyond that gate.
Ten thousand saints have called the odds,
wagered their substance on a spring

resembling that April we saw,
long ago, when growth was part of life,
accepted like the air and mother earth.

BY THE SAME AUTHOR

Collections of poetry
Swords of the Kingdom	1961
Beating Wings	1965
The Poem of Existence	1971
The Following Spring	1980
The Valley of Dry Bones	1985
The Warp and the Weft	1986
Clouds of Glory	1994*
Words for Worship	1995*

Religious Education
A series of twelve books for children entitled *Learning about Religion*   1979

Theological works
The Treasures of Jesus	1994*
Tongues of Angels	1994*
The Six-Chaplet Rosary	1994*
The Treasures of Saint Paul	1995*
365 Days with the Psalms (co-author)	1996*

Articles in *Vetus Testamentum* and *Zeitschrift für die Alttestamentliche Wissenschaft*

* Published by ST PAULS